AF413526

FRICTION AND THE LAWS OF MOTION PHYSICS MADE SIMPLE

4th Grade

Children's Physics Books

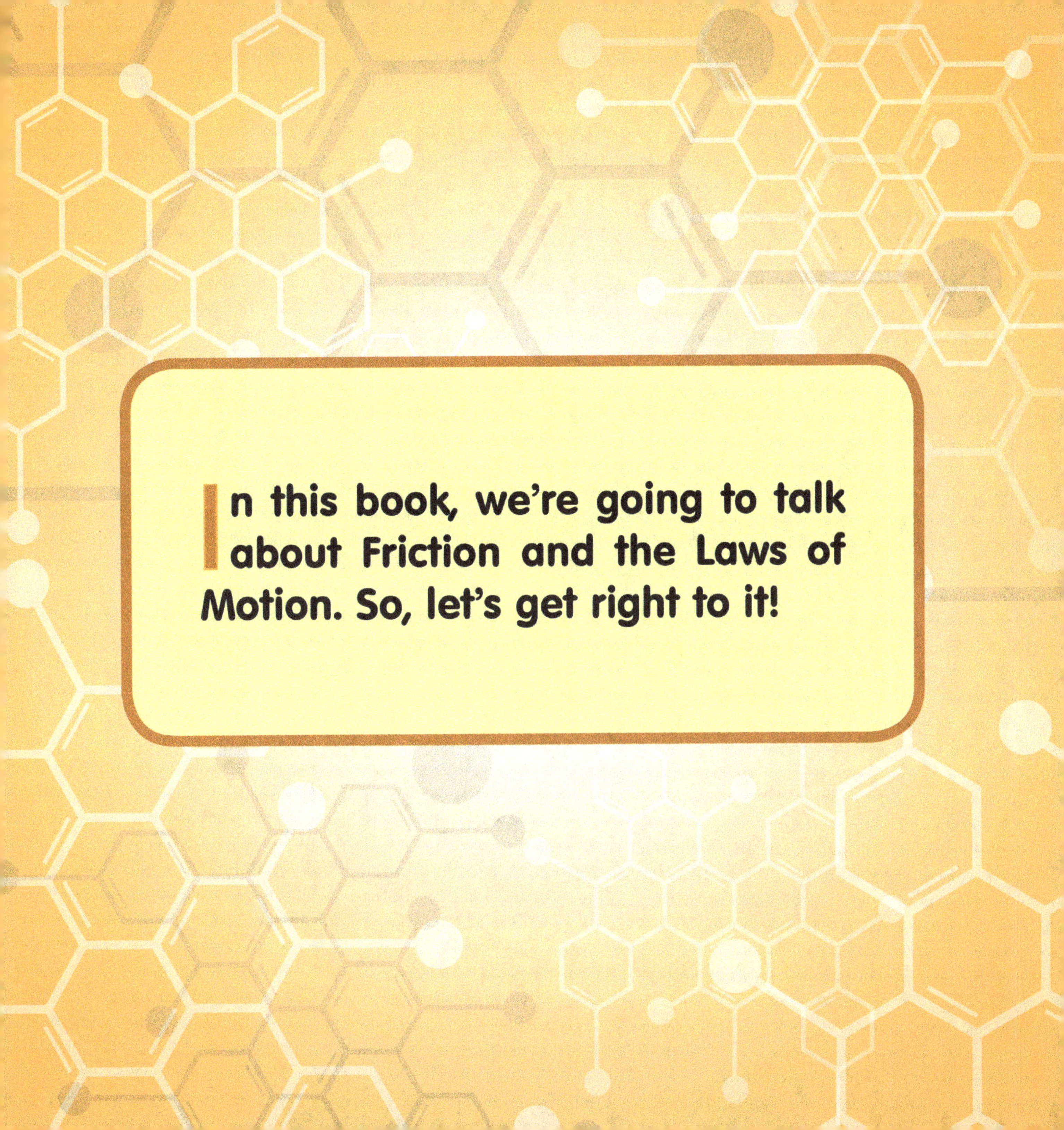
In this book, we're going to talk about Friction and the Laws of Motion. So, let's get right to it!

Sir Isaac Newton

The three laws of motion that Sir Isaac Newton, the famous physicist, stated over three centuries ago might seem like common sense today. However, when he first proposed them, they were thought to be a revolution in scientific thought.

His concepts became the foundation for the study of physics.

At the beginning, Newton was studying the motion of the planets. He began to describe how these huge planets and other celestial objects would behave when forces, such as gravity, influenced them. To formulate his laws, Newton had three important factors— the mass of an object, the length it travels, and the time period it takes.

A stationary golf ball.

NEWTON'S FIRST LAW OF MOTION

Newton's first law of motion tells us that if an object is stationary it will remain that way unless a force is applied to it. Also, an object that's in motion will stay that way unless a force prevents it from staying in motion.

When an object stays at rest, we say that it's in a state of "inertia." Newton's law means that an object doesn't suddenly stop, completely change directions, or start moving all by itself. Some force must act upon the object to get it to move.

Let's look at this first law of motion with a simple example. Suppose you have a ball on the ground. The ball will remain motionless or in a state of inertia unless you do something to it.

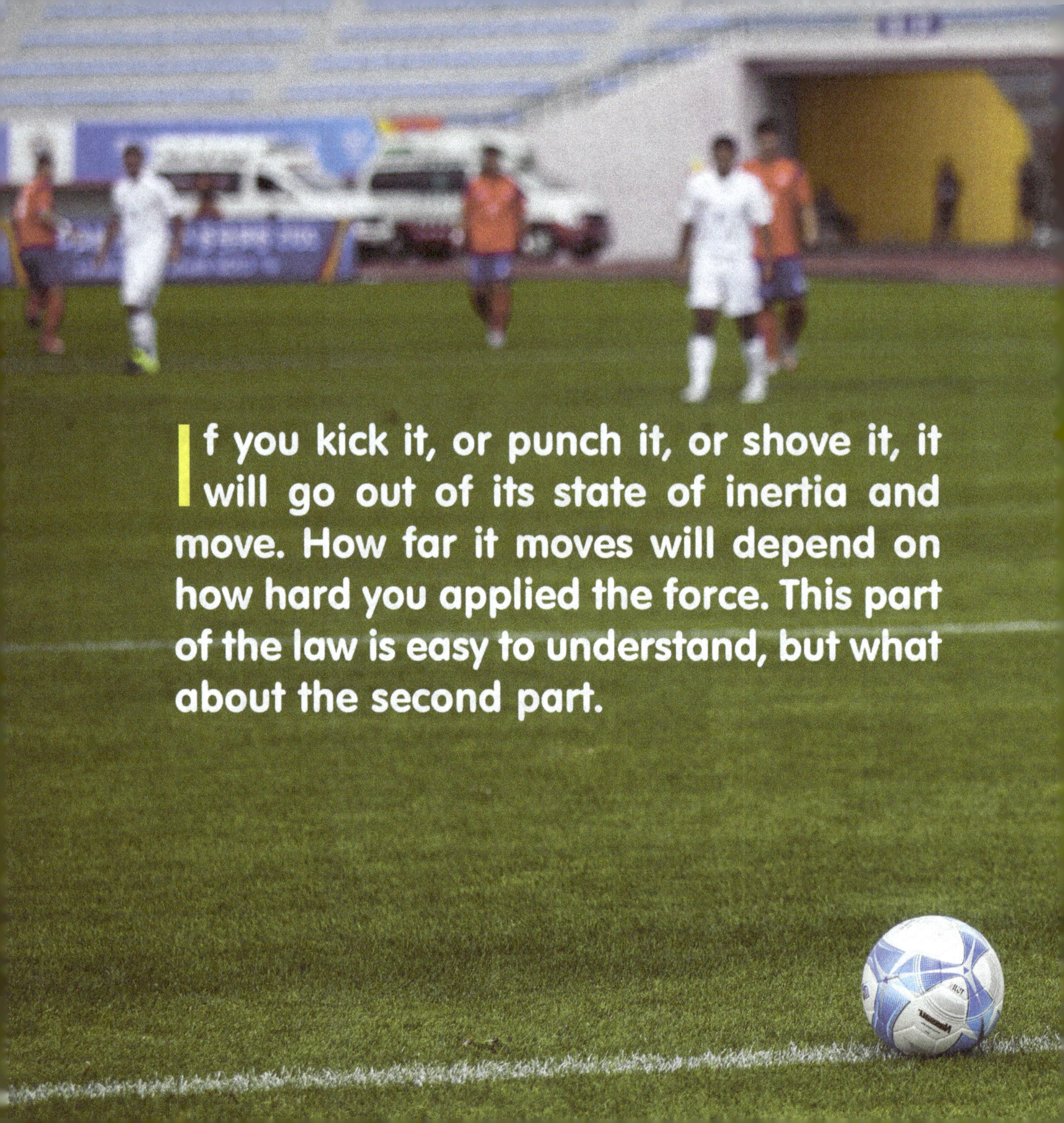

If you kick it, or punch it, or shove it, it will go out of its state of inertia and move. How far it moves will depend on how hard you applied the force. This part of the law is easy to understand, but what about the second part.

Once you kick the ball, you don't expect it to continue to remain in motion. But, why doesn't it? That's because there are unseen forces that apply to the motion of the ball. There's the force of the Earth that pulls on the ball. That force is called gravity.

There are also things like friction from the air and from the ground. So unless the ball is in an environment where none of these things exist, eventually it's going to stop. It won't roll away from your kick and continue forever and ever.

WHAT IS FRICTION?

You encounter friction of all types in daily life. Whenever one object rubs against another friction happens. Friction works against whatever motion is happening and pushes the object in the opposite direction.

Writing creates friction

The friction creates heat when you rub your hands together to get warm.

HOW DOES FRICTION INFLUENCE ENERGY?

A good example of friction and energy is when you rub the palms of your hands together. If it's cold out, you might do that to keep your hands warm.

The friction of rubbing your hands together has changed the energy of your movement, which is called kinetic energy, to heat, another type of energy. Remember energy is never destroyed.

Instead, it's just converted from one type of energy to another.

Let's say you have heavy boxes that you want to slide down a ramp. As the boxes start to slide they encounter resistance. That resistance is the friction from the box and ramp rubbing against each other. The box starts to slow down because the force of friction is hampering its movement.

Sliding creates friction

SUSHI

HOW CAN FRICTION BE PREVENTED?

In order for us to make our work easier, we've invented ways to reduce the amount of friction. For example, we might use a dolly, which is a flat cart with wheels, to move the heavy box or a piece of furniture. The wheels help reduce the frictional resistance of the ramp.

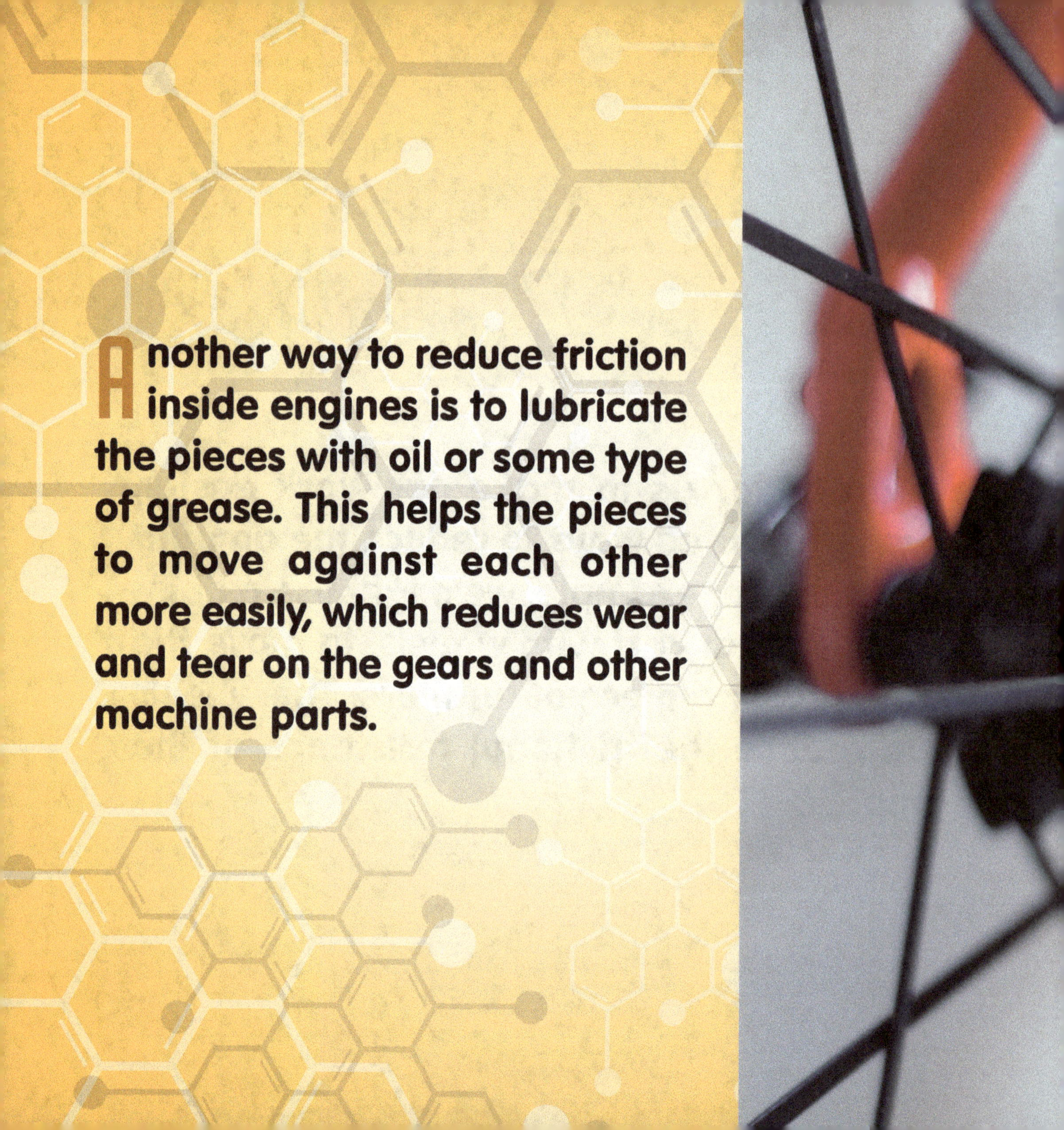

Another way to reduce friction inside engines is to lubricate the pieces with oil or some type of grease. This helps the pieces to move against each other more easily, which reduces wear and tear on the gears and other machine parts.

A third way to minimize friction is to change the materials that are rubbing against each other. If you practice ice-skating, you know that the steel on your ice skates slides very well on the ice. There's some resistance from the friction, but not enough to resist your sliding along gracefully as you start to skate.

H owever, if you wear rubber shoes on a sidewalk, there's a lot of friction between the material of rubber and the material of concrete so it keeps you from slipping, which is what you want in this case! Different types of materials have different types of "friction coefficients" in relationship to each other.

TRY SOME EXPERIMENTS WITH FRICTION

Try putting some objects with different types of surfaces on a tray. Then, lift the tray in the air and just tilt it very slightly to one side. The material with the least friction compared to the surface friction will begin to slide and will slide faster than the others.

For example, if you have a smooth rock and a bumpy rock of similar masses, the bumpy rock will have more resistance with the smooth tray so it will not slide as fast as the smooth rock will. Force, of course, makes a difference too. The more you angle the tray, the more quickly the objects will slide down due to the angle and the force of gravity.

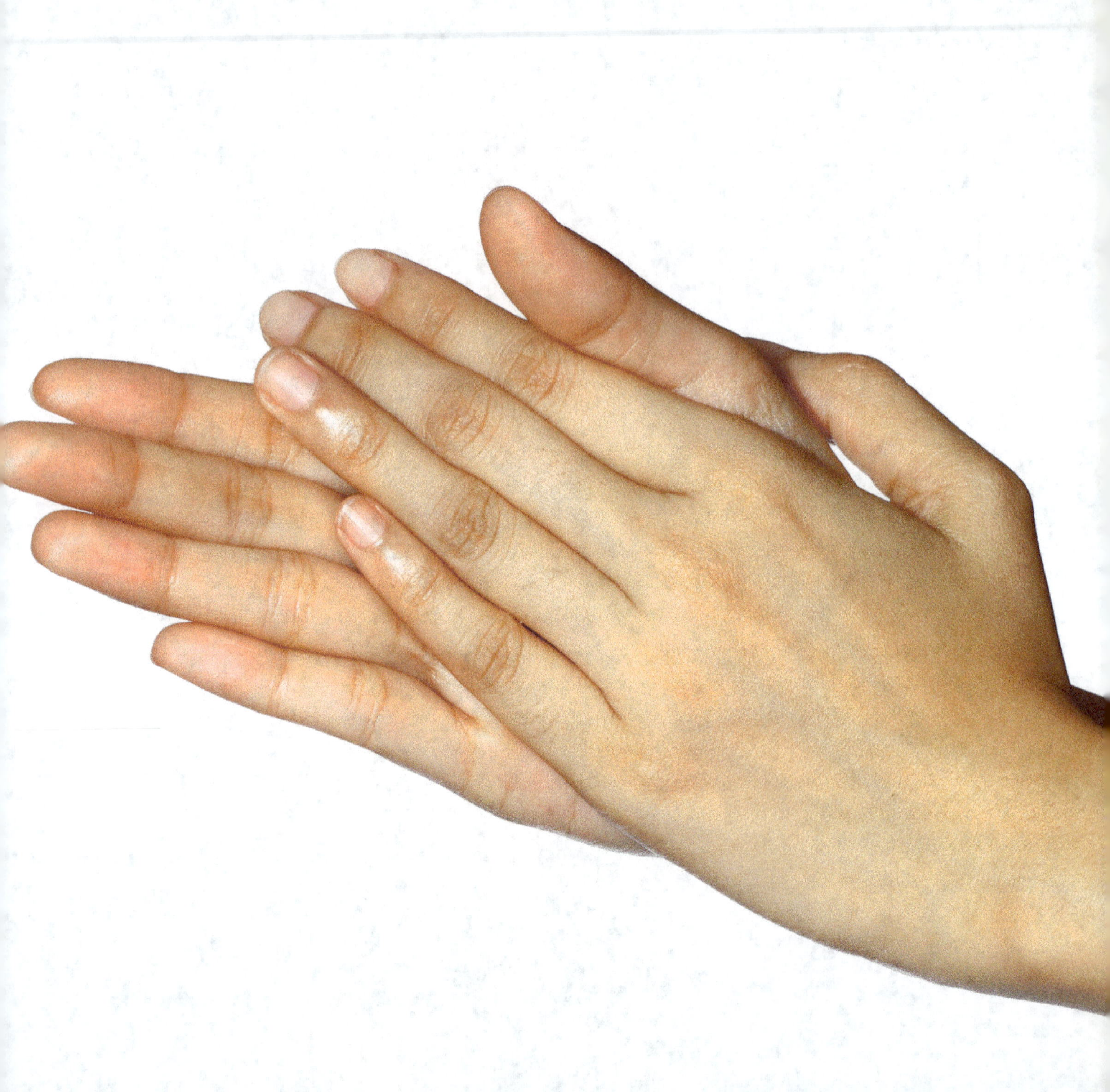

TYPES OF FRICTION

DRY FRICTION

When two objects that have dry surfaces are up against each other, that's an example of static friction. An example of static friction would be if you pressed your palms together but didn't move them at all. However, if you rubbed your palms together that would be an example of two surfaces moving against each other. This type of friction is called kinetic friction or sliding friction.

FLUID FRICTION

Fluid friction involves friction with currents, such as currents of air or water. A boat moving in water is an example of fluid friction and so is an airplane that's encountering the resistance of air currents.

ROLLING FRICTION

In our earlier example, we placed the heavy box on a dolly or hand truck to roll it. This is an example of rolling friction. Without balls or wheels, moving things from place to place would be so much harder!

NEWTON'S SECOND LAW OF MOTION

Newton's second law tells us that the greater an object's mass, the more force it's going to take to move it and make it move faster. That means the force it's going to take to get a toy rocket to go up in the air and accelerate as it gets off the ground is going to be a lot less than the amazing amounts of force it takes to get a real rocket off the ground!

The equation for force is Force = mass times acceleration, which in symbols is $F = ma$. Friction plays a part here as well. A rocket will have to overcome the friction of the atmosphere before it gets out into space.

NEWTON'S THIRD LAW OF MOTION

The third law states that for each action, there's an opposite action that takes place. This essentially means that forces come in pairs. If you sit in a chair, your body is forcing you downwards. If the chair doesn't have any upward force to act against your force, it would collapse under you and not be able to support your weight.

THE BOBBSEY TWINS AT THE COUNTY FAIR

When a gun fires a bullet, the force of the bullet going out causes the gun to move backwards. Friction also has an impact on all forces and it moves in an opposite direction to the force. For example, the bullet as it is fired from the inside of a gun rubs against the inside barrel on its way out. The force of the gun has to be powerful enough for the bullet to fly out.

SOME INTERESTING THINGS ABOUT FRICTION, FORCE AND NEWTON'S LAWS OF MOTION

Friction prevents us from getting from place to place as fast as we'd like to, but without friction lots of things wouldn't work.

Even though wheels are designed to reduce friction, friction makes it possible for them to work too.

Coins

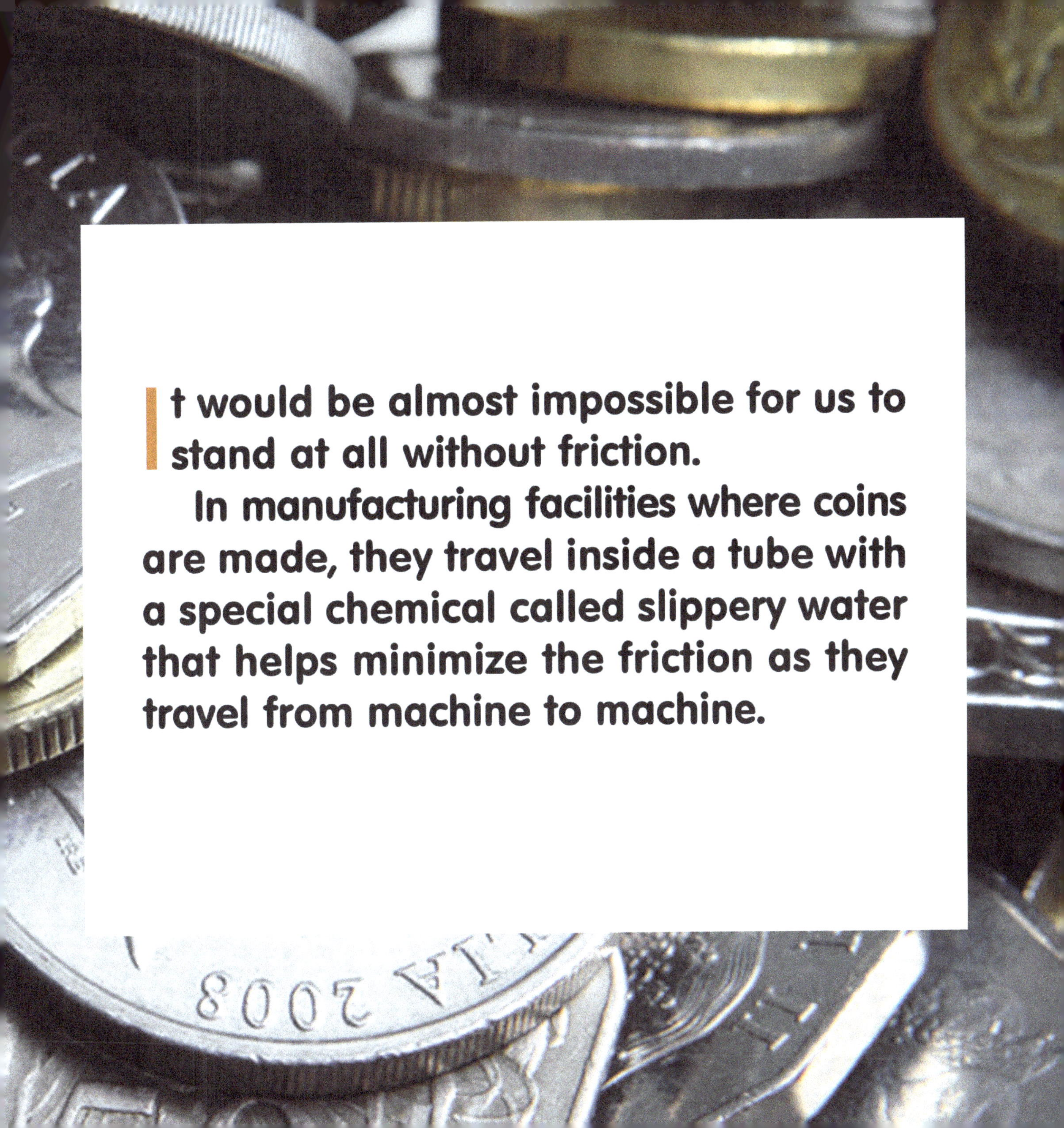

It would be almost impossible for us to stand at all without friction.

In manufacturing facilities where coins are made, they travel inside a tube with a special chemical called slippery water that helps minimize the friction as they travel from machine to machine.

f two surfaces are pressed hard together, it's very difficult to get them to slide.

In water parks, fluid friction is used to
make it possible for us to glide smoothly
and quickly down the giant slides.

NEWTON

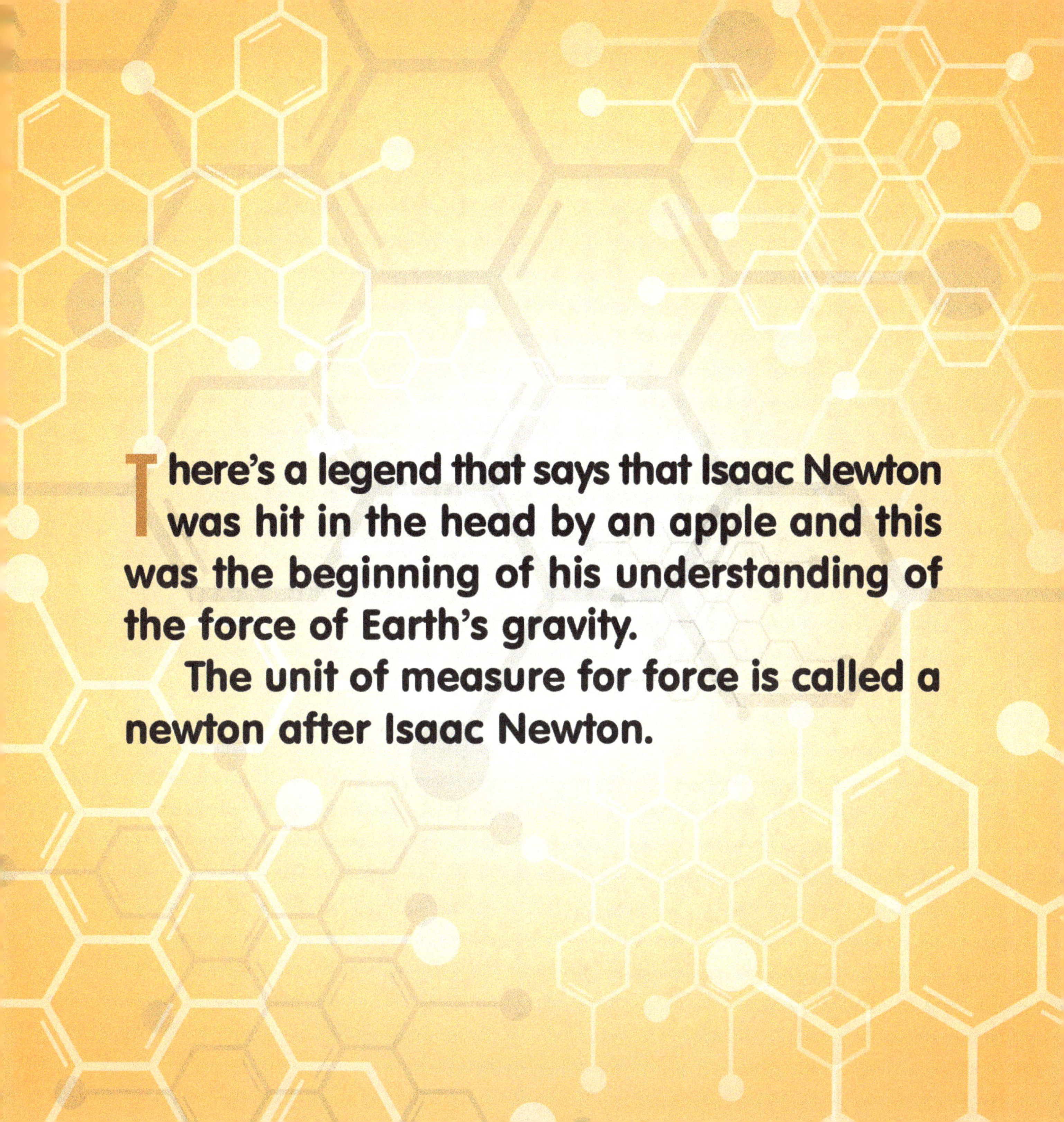

There's a legend that says that Isaac Newton was hit in the head by an apple and this was the beginning of his understanding of the force of Earth's gravity.

The unit of measure for force is called a newton after Isaac Newton.

All gases as well as liquids use equal force in every direction they travel. This law, called Pascal's Law, was named after the famous scientist and mathematician Blaise Pascal.

Blaise Pascal

If you've ever traveled very fast in a looping roller coaster, you know that you feel a force keeping you in your seat so you won't fall out. It's a special type of force called centripetal force. You should still stay strapped in though!

Awesome! Now you know more about the different types of friction and the Laws of Motion. You can find more Physics books from Baby Professor by searching the website of your favorite book retailer.

Visit

BABY PROFESSOR
EDUCATION KIDS

www.BabyProfessorBooks.com

to download Free Baby Professor eBooks and view
our catalog of new and exciting Children's Books